God Renews Our
Relationships
With Others

God Renews Our
Relationships
With Others

Volume 2

By
Farley Dunn

THIS IS A MYCHURCHNOTES.NET BOOK

PUBLISHED BY MYCHURCHNOTES.NET
AND THREE SKILLET PUBLISHING
(www.ThreeSkilletPublishing.com)

COPYRIGHT © 2017 BY FARLEY DUNN

www.MyChurchNotes.net

God Renews Our Relationships with Others/Farley Dunn
1st ed.

Vol. 2

This is an original work created by
Farley Dunn for the website MyChurchNotes.net.

All rights reserved.

ISBN: 978-1-943189-40-3

Non-public domain scripture quotations are from The Holy Bible, English Standard Version® (ESV®), copyright © 2001 by Crossway, a publishing ministry of Good News Publishers. Used by permission. All rights reserved.

Dedication

To Trudy.

Twice, life hit our family a blow,
and you were there for us.

MyChurchNotes.net

Table of Contents

Barber Shop Quartet	19
Beggars' Robes Cast Aside	25
Building a Better Billboard	31
Chunkin' Punkins	37
Corrupted in the Eyes of God	43
Finding Our Love Zone	49
Flagged for Jesus	55
Getting a God Hug	61
Getting on the Good Side of Our Problems	67
High-Voltage Christianity	73
Identity Confirmed	79
I Know Your Works	87
Linked by Love	93
Living Bald-Headed for God	99
Lost in Translation	105
One for Jesus; Jesus for All	111
Punching Up the Package	117
Purple and Fine Linen	125
Refer-a-Friend	131
Running With Jesus	139
Setting Up Our Wall	145
The Beautiful Sin	151
The Hand-Carved Beam	157
The Sparrow's Wingbeat	161
The Weaving Machine	167
Tit for Tat	175
Wagons Westward Ho!	183
Coming to Christ in Three Easy Steps	187

Introduction

Others find Jesus through us.

His earthly hand is found in the flesh of ours. Without our muscles, sinews, and bones, the saving message of our Lord falls flat. No one will hear it, because we're not there to live it out for them.

The Holy Word of God is expressed through us.

How?

We live out God's Word in the way we interact with those around us. How do we respond to hurt, intentional or otherwise, or slights to our sense of self-importance? Do pinpricks of pain turn into slashing blows of cruelty, or are we overly sensitive because we're having a bad day, and we forget others have them, too?

In "Finding Our Love Zone," read about living in the sweet spot where we can let people be more important than our possessions. "Purple and Fine

Linen" is our reminder to treat our fellow travelers as God's children. "The Weaving Machine" reveals the differences in each of us, and that God treasures us for that very reason.

When we step away from *us* and step into the shoes of *others,* the world will be forever changed, and the lost will find Jesus in us.

Farley Dunn

Light Bulb Moment

When we present ourselves as the envoy of Christ, let's make sure we are prepared for the part.

Barber Shop Quartet

SINGING IN A quartet is rather an old-fashioned thing to do in today's modern world. There are several groups that still manage to pull this off. Don't picture the rag-tag, oddly-dressed people that pervade the edgy music scene of today's youth. Rather, these men dress to the nines, and they present themselves shaved and trimmed to perfection.

One of these is the Irish Tenors, a trio of men who are world renowned for their musical excellence. True, they are a trio rather than a quartet, but the effect is the same. They join voices, each providing a different part of the total experience, and the result is astounding.

The Gaither Vocal Band has five members. They sing in suits and ties, and they present both a polished look and an enjoyable performance. We never have to worry they are unprepared. In their presentation, they are everything we expect them to be, from the shoes on their feet, to the cut of their hair.

God wants us to be a quartet of magnificent beauty, both in our appearance, and in our interactions with each other and the world. He knows if we are sloppy in appearance, the world will see us as sloppy in our walk with God.

- ➢ Leviticus 19:27 tells us that our beauty is perfect the way God created us. We need to love ourselves as we are, and in doing so, we will love our fellow singers as well.
- ➢ Leviticus 21:5 lets us know that marring our bodies distracts others from hearing our message of holiness. It is in our moderation of dress and action that others see the strength in our song.
- ➢ Isaiah 50:6 says there are those who will find fault with our appearance, no matter what we do. Yet, if we sing Jesus' song, our voices will rise ever more sweetly before our holy Lord.
- ➢ Jeremiah 49:32 is God's scornful view of the one who tries to improve upon what God has already made perfect. We will be kicked off the stage, if we try to outshine those who sing with us.

- Ezekiel 44:20 is a call to moderation in our appearance, to be neither scruffy nor elaborately flamboyant. Our dress must enhance our quartet rather than pull the world's attention from the message of the Christ.
- Proverbs 20:29 wants us to find pride in the years of our experience, and to let those years speak of the wisdom we have learned. It is the gray-haired Christian who adds the sweetest note to the song.
- Psalm 133:2 describes God's magnificence flowing over us when we sing in unison with our brothers.
- 2 Samuel 19:24 is about our pardon. We are in disgrace until we come on God's stage with our appearance slicked up and ready for him. Only then can we sing along in his magnificent heavenly quartet.
- Leviticus 14:9 is our symbol of purification. When the world has made us filthy, we must cast it all off to become pure for God. We have no choice, if we are to sing with him.

In our Christian walk, we are not soloists. We sing one line of notes, and it is those at our side that fill in the rest of the melody, harmonizing, sometimes adding a dissonant chord, but always lifting the beauty of the song to those who are watching us perform on the stage of life. Let's present ourselves well, so that the world will want to sing along with us.

When we present ourselves as the envoy of Christ, let's make sure we are prepared for the part.

Light Bulb Moment

Our true colors are seen in our spirit. Let's be a rainbow for the Lord.

Beggars' Robes Cast Aside

NOT ALL BEGGARS are poor. Massu in India hires a taxi to his begging spot, dons his ragged clothes, and works hard for eight hours. Afterwards, he changes again and hires a taxi home.

He also owns property valued at around $750,000 in 2015 U.S. dollars.

When Massu sheds his begging robes, he becomes the person he really is, a prosperous businessman with money in the bank.

As Christians, we need to cast our begging robes aside and become the people we really are. We are rich in the blessings of our Lord, and we need to live in our wealth.

1 John 1:9 tells us:

"If we confess our sins, he is faithful and just to

forgive us our sins and to cleanse us from all unrighteousness."

Bank account full! We are wealthy with righteousness.

Romans 6:23 tells us:

"For the wages of sin is death, but the free gift of God is eternal life in Christ Jesus our Lord."

Retirement accounts fully funded! We don't have to worry about the future.

John 3:16-17 tells us:

"For God so loved the world, that he gave his only Son, that whoever believes in him should not perish but have eternal life. For God did not send his Son into the world to condemn the world, but in order that the world might be saved through him."

We have enough to share! Let's invite our fellow man into God's riches.

1 Peter 3:18 tells us:

"For Christ also suffered once for sins, the righteous for the unrighteous, that he might bring us to God, being put to death in the flesh but made alive in the spirit."

Our wealth is in our spirit! We forget sometimes that the world is not our home. It's not big houses and fancy cars that are our Christian heritage. Rather, we are rich in love for our fellow man, and when we show the love of Christ to those around us, they will share in our wealth.

So, let's quit begging. No more Poor, Poor, Pitiful Me! We live in excess! Let's jump for joy and rejoice in Jesus, our Savior and King.

Our true colors are seen in our spirit. Let's be a rainbow for the Lord.

Light Bulb Moment

When people see the cross, they are reminded of every time they have spoken to a Christian. We are Christ to them, for it is through us that Jesus shows his divine nature to the world.

Building a Better Billboard

SOME ADVERTISING LOGOS have become iconic. No matter where we are in the world or in what media we see that familiar shape, we know the product.

And chances are, we trust it simply because it is so familiar.

Take the undulating bottle Coca-Cola has trademarked. All we have to see is part of that outline, and we know what we're looking at beyond a shadow of a doubt. There is the Nike Swoosh. Whole television commercials have been produced with no mention of Nike's name. Yet, at the end, we see the Swoosh, and we instantly connect the advertisement with the product.

That connection in our thoughts is what makes advertising logos so vital to business. It is the reason companies will spend millions of dollars to build product identity, and then maintain that iconic emblem for another fifty years. It has become them.

Take Mazda. A number of years ago they started a new ad campaign showing a fast car on a winding road, and a boy appeared, whispering, "Zoom, zoom."

Those two words became iconic for Mazda. Mazda no longer uses that boy in its commercials, but listen carefully, and when we see a Mazda ad on television today, at the end, we hear those two familiar words, "Zoom, zoom." That's brand imagery, and it connects us to all those other commercials.

What is our advertising logo for Jesus? The obvious one is the cross.

A single cross placed in any location, no matter how unusual, clearly stands for Jesus. Across the world, the symbol is ubiquitous.

Those three crosses raised high on Golgotha's hill? When we see those symbolic cruciform images, no matter how basic the representation, a connection is instantly there. They have become the billboard for the church.

Yet, what are we really telling the unchurched with our billboard? What do they really see when that cross is raised high? Do they envision an event that occurred two thousand years ago? Or do they see the representation of Christ in us? When they see the cross, are they reminded of Shawn across the street offering to mow their lawn when they were down with the flu? Or maybe they think of the Fall Fun Festival we invited their children to. Perhaps it's seeing the taillights of our car as we faithfully leave for church each Sunday morning.

Proverbs is a treasure trove of advertising ideas. If we remember the following four suggestions, those around us will see the hand of Christ in our lives:

> Suggestion #1: Proverbs 21:20 reveals that the wise use of our resources is a godly example to those around us.

> Suggestion #2: Proverbs 28:22 tells us that stinginess will create a bad reputation.

> Suggestion #3: Proverbs 22:16 warns us against putting our desire for money above our concern for those we come into contact with every day.

> Suggestion #4: Proverbs 16:33 reminds us that even when we think we have control of everything, it is really God that directs the fall of the dice.

The New Testament gives us two additional ways

we can boldly advertise for Christ. Let's look at these iconic ideals that every Christian should strive for:

> Ideal #1: James 2:19 espouses that our professed belief in God is essential.
>
> Ideal #2: Matthew 5:42 encourages us to be generous with those in need.

What brand imagery do we show to the world? We are all billboards for Christ, whether we like it or not, and every action we take, every interaction with another human, creates an image that will live on long past the moment we walk away from that situation. When people see an image of a cross on the hill, what they really see is us and how we presented Christ to them.

We need to make that advertising moment a positive one, and we can only do that by following the instructions we find in the Word of God.

When people see the cross, they are reminded of every time they have spoken to a Christian. We are Christ to them, for it is through us that Jesus shows his divine nature to the world.

Light Bulb Moment

When we're chunkin' punkins, we're sending our anger as far from us as possible. Then we win, God wins, and our fellow man also wins.

Chunkin' Punkins

THERE'S A SPORT that takes pumpkins—the Halloween kind—and sees just how far we can toss those round, orange fruits.

The competition is so fevered, some teams resort to building massive trebuchets to send their orange bombs as far into the field as possible.

Why trebuchets? Simply, there is a bucket or loop on one end to hold the little orange beastie, and the weight on the other end can be wound as tightly as desired to build up as much force as possible. Then, when the trebuchet's giant arm swings around, launching the pumpkin forward, it flies through the air with the greatest of ease.

Now, some people might read this and think, "Oh, what a waste of a good pumpkin!"

True. However, pumpkins are grown in massive

quantities, and if they are not used in a timely manner, they spoil and become a smelly nuisance. A rotten pumpkin is something no one wants around.

What are the rotten pumpkins we fail to load into our trebuchets as Christians? Ah, now we're to the meat of our article. There are things we need to cast as far from us as possible, because they will pollute our walk with Jesus.

Let's look at seven examples from the Word of God:

Example #1:

> Psalm 37:8 tells us: "Refrain from anger, and forsake wrath! Fret not yourself; it tends only to evil."
>
> Chunk that punkin!

Example #2:

> Proverbs 14:29 reminds us: "Whoever is slow to anger has great understanding, but he who has a hasty temper exalts folly."
>
> Chunk that punkin!

Example #3:

James 1:20 cautions us: "For the anger of man does not produce the righteousness of God."

Chunk that punkin!

Example #4:

Ecclesiastes 7:9 is our guide: "Be not quick in your spirit to become angry, for anger lodges in the bosom of fools."

Chunk that punkin!

Example #5:

James 1:19 directs us: "Know this, my beloved brothers: let every person be quick to hear, slow to speak, slow to anger."

Chunk that punkin!

Example #6:

Proverbs 15:1 is all about our tongue: "A soft answer turns away wrath, but a harsh word stirs up anger."

Chunk that punkin!

Example #7:

Ephesians 4:31 lays it out for us boldly and without question: "Let all bitterness and wrath and anger and clamor and slander be put away from you, along with all malice."

Chunk that punkin!

What pumpkins does God wish us to load into our trebuchets? Our anger, of course. If we fail to get it as far from us as possible, our anger will rot within us, and we will become a sour stink in the nostrils of God.

When we're chunkin' punkins, we're sending our anger as far from us as possible. Then we win, God wins, and our fellow man also wins.

Light Bulb Moment

When we step out without God's approval, we step into a minefield of unimaginable proportions.

Corrupted in the Eyes of God

AT THE ONSET of World War II, many countries became one. Their concessions of freedom weren't voluntary.

In 1938 a portion of Czechoslovakia was annexed into Germany. In 1939, Hitler seized the rest. That same year, more confident, Hitler made a grab for Poland and took it for his own.

At first it seemed Hitler would rule much of the world. At the height of his power, one hand reached toward the British Isles and the other squeezed Russia's throat.

Truth caught up with Hitler, though. Conquest by force is infused with corruption, and it can never become a true marriage between people, races, or countries. It just doesn't work.

We see this principle in the Bible. Deuteronomy 22:28-29 tells us that if a man makes a grab for a woman and takes her before marriage, the relationship is corrupted. He has violated her and must marry her, paying a substantial bride price.

It becomes a forced marriage, and who wants to be a part of that?

Genesis 34:1-31 tells the story of Jacob's daughter, Dinah. Shechem, a prince of the land, loved Dinah and took her without the sanctity of marriage. Afterward he begged for her hand in marriage.

It seemed that true love had blossomed. Even so, the union was corrupted, and all the males in the city—including Shechem—were killed by Dinah's brothers.

The story of Absalom and Tamar in 2 Samuel 13:1-39 is the classic biblical example of a corrupted conquest gone as wrong as it possibly can. Absalom and Tamar were siblings, and Tamar was very beautiful. Another sibling, Amnon, took his sister through guile and lies. The eventual outcome? Absalom killed his brother and afterward spent years on the run. The corruption of Amnon's deed planted a seed of contention in Absalom against his father, David the king, and in a grab for the kingship, he was killed by Joab, David's top man.

The corrupted conquest didn't stop there, though. Years later, in 1 Kings 2, on David's deathbed, the king instructed Solomon, the upcoming king, to deal with Joab in the harshest way possible. Joab was David's most trusted warrior, a supporter of the king for all his days, but corruption had taken its toll, for that is what corruption does.

Hitler's Third Reich was to last a thousand years. It barely made it through the first ten before the corrupted leader of the German people died by suicide, with his body burned beyond recognition in the final rubble of the worldly palace he'd tried to build.

If our conquests are not sanctified by God, they will not stand; rather, they will come tumbling down, no more than piles of rubble crumpled beneath clouds of rising dust soon carried away by the wind.

When we step out without God's approval, we step into a minefield of unimaginable proportions.

Light Bulb Moment

When we orbit God, we will draw others to him.

Finding Our Love Zone

LOOK UP ON a clear night. The number of stars overhead boggles the imagination. There are a billion billion tiny pinpoints of light up there, each one a fiery, burning star akin to our sun.

One thing we can't see just by looking up is that most of them are binary star systems. That means two or more stars rotate around each other, putting two suns in the skies of each planet.

Take the star system named Kepler-47. It has a primary sun (the larger of the two) and a secondary sun. They orbit each other every 7.5 days. They sling a solitary planet through an ellipse that takes it from just about where Venus orbits our sun to just past the position of Earth.

That's important, because it's what scientists call the "habitable zone." We could rename it the Goldilocks zone: Not too close, and not too far away for life to be possible. The Earth falls in the Goldilocks zone around our sun, and that's why our atmosphere doesn't get ripped away by the fierce solar winds, and the water in our oceans remains in liquid form.

We must find the Goldilocks zone in our personal lives, also. It's the zone where the people around us aren't scorched by our possessive need to own them, yet they aren't frozen out by our indifference.

We must keep people in our love zone.

1 John 4:7-8 defines what goes on in our love zone. When we let people inside, they will feel the joy of God emanating from us in everything we do.

> "Beloved, let us love one another, for love is from God, and whoever loves has been born of God and knows God. Anyone who does not love does not know God, because God is love."

Colossians 3:12 paints a picture of the beauty that will draw people into our love zone. When they see us reflecting the awesomeness of God, they will know it's safe to be at our side.

> "Put on then, as God's chosen ones, holy and beloved, compassionate hearts, kindness, humility,

meekness, and patience . . ."

Matthew 17:5 gives people a strong signal the dispossessed can lock onto. When we tout the truth of Christ, they will know we offer them safety in our love zone.

> "He was still speaking when, behold, a bright cloud overshadowed them, and a voice from the cloud said, 'This is my beloved Son, with whom I am well pleased; listen to him.' "

1 John 3:1-2 explains why some people are still landing on desolate and uninhabitable worlds searching for reassurance that someone cares. They are looking for love where it cannot be found. We need to raise our banners higher so that they can find our love zone.

> "See what kind of love the Father has given to us, that we should be called children of God; and so we are. The reason why the world does not know us is that it did not know him. Beloved, we are God's children now, and what we will be has not yet appeared; but we know that when he appears we shall be like him, because we shall see him as he is."

We need to be Kepler-47s for Jesus. He is our primary star, our eternal source of power, controlling everything we do. We are secondary to him, orbiting him closely and at a phenomenal speed. When we let ourselves be drawn into this tightly-knit configuration, the poor, the lost, and the hurting will be pulled into our love zone, and they will find eternal peace in the love of our Holy God.

When we orbit God, we will draw others to him.

Light Bulb Moment

When we carry Christ's flag, people will look for Jesus in us.

Flagged for Jesus

WHEN WE WANT to mark something, we flag it.

Sprinkler heads in the yard? Flagged. Boundaries for the new highway? Flagged. U.S. Post Office? Flagged. Military company? Flagged.

We know where these things are, and even what they are, because of the flags we use. Dig and find an unmarked sprinkler head, and we've got a gusher of water when the system turns on. That highway can't be built across just any field. And the U.S. flag? That speaks over two hundred years of history. We're proud of that.

What about spiritual flags? Do we have them? Are they out for people to see?

Exodus 17:15 tells us:

> "And Moses built an altar and called the name of it, The Lord Is My Banner . . ."

If people dig where we are, they should find the power of the Lord gushing forth. Our flag needs to announce our connection to everyone we come into contact with.

John 8:32 says:

"And you will know the truth, and the truth will set you free."

This verse talks about the highway to Heaven. We want it flagged as prominently as possible so that everyone can get on.

John 1:1-5 gives us the history behind our flag:

"In the beginning was the Word, and the Word was with God, and the Word was God. He was in the beginning with God. All things were made through him, and without him was not anything made that was made. In him was life, and the life was the light of men. The light shines in the darkness, and the darkness has not overcome it."

That passage should make us stand at attention with our hands in a salute, and pride should fill us up. Jesus, the Christ, our Everlasting Redeemer was there at the beginning of all creation, and he shines still today, in spite of the darkness that tries to envelop the world. How wonderful is that?

There's one more flag we must pay attention to. It's the one that marks the casket of a veteran. It tells us that the person inside didn't just talk the talk; he or she walked the walk, a true member of our country's military juggernaut, a person who risked life and limb to bring peace and security to the world.

Let's make sure we, as Christians, earn the right to be flagged for Jesus in that final hour. We want the world to know we risked life and limb to bring Christ and the message of the cross to the world.

When we carry Christ's flag, people will look for Jesus in us.

Light Bulb Moment

Let's have a hug fest, with us in the middle surrounded by the Father, the Son, and the Spirit. Then we'll really feel the love.

Getting a God Hug

HUMANS ARE built to form emotional attachments. It's what bonds mothers to their children, and keeps families together for half a century.

That old saying, someone only a mother could love? It's truer than true. A mother will love, because the attachment is so strong not even a wicked child can shatter it.

Sometimes the attachment never happens, and that's when trouble sets in. The mother never bonds with her baby, and she sees the child as a burden rather than a blessing. If a child doesn't bond with an adult, we get Reactive Attachment Disorder (RAD). The child's ability to interact properly with others is affected, creating issues such as learning difficulties and emotional problems throughout the child's life.

One suggested treatment for small children with

RAD is to establish a regular schedule to hold them.

We need to give the child a hug.

Is it possible for us to get SRAD? That's Spiritual Reactive Attachment Disorder. Of course that's not a real diagnosis, but it could be. We all know people who have the symptoms. They haven't bonded with God, and they have trouble learning how he wants them to live. Some even rant and rave at God when they don't get their way.

SRAD. Spiritual Reactive Attachment Disorder. How do we cure it?

God gives us a hug.

The big hug comes in John 3:16:

> "For God so loved the world, that he gave his only Son, that whoever believes in him should not perish but have eternal life."

How's that for the Almighty Creator reaching out to us to give us that touch of his presence that we so desperately need?

Here are some more:

Ephesians 2:8 tells us:

"For by grace you have been saved through faith. And this is not your own doing; it is the gift of God."

Jeremiah 29:13 tells how we can hug him back:

"You will seek me and find me, when you seek me with all your heart."

Luke 1:37 encourages us:

"For nothing will be impossible with God."

Mark 11:24 says how easy it is:

"Therefore I tell you, whatever you ask in prayer, believe that you have received it, and it will be yours."

John 15:9 gives us our finest example:

"As the Father has loved me, so have I loved you. Abide in my love."

In 1 Peter 3:18-22 we find one of God's historic hug highlights compared to the resurrection of Jesus:

"For Christ also suffered once for sins, the righteous for the unrighteous, that he might bring us to God, being put to death in the flesh but made alive in the spirit, in which he went and proclaimed to the spirits in prison, because they formerly did not obey, when God's patience waited in the days of Noah, while the ark was being prepared, in which a few, that is, eight persons, were brought safely through water.

"Baptism, which corresponds to this, now saves you, not as a removal of dirt from the body but as an appeal to God for a good conscience, through the resurrection of Jesus Christ, who has gone into heaven and is at the right hand of God, with angels, authorities, and powers having been subjected to him."

When God hugs us, we become bonded to him. All he wants is for us to hug him back, and we do that through our praises to him.

Let's have a hug fest, with us in the middle surrounded by the Father, the Son, and the Spirit. Then we'll really feel the love.

Light Bulb Moment

Jesus is our number one authority, and the only thing he tells us to do is love one another.

Getting on the Good Side of our Problems

ENGLISH TEACHERS shudder at the use of inappropriately used words. When we turn a noun into a verb, chills run up and down their spines.

For example, here's a well-known noun used as a verb in business meetings: When a discussion can't be resolved, we table it. It means to put it aside for a time.

More recently, we Facebook someone. It means to contact them through the social media site.

Even worse for English teachers is using an adverb as a verb. Good, better, and best describe the condition of something. For some of us, lemon pies are good, apple is better, but pecan is the best of all.

We never hear someone say they will good themselves, but we can best an opponent. On a personal level, we can better our lot in life.

How can we better ourselves underneath the guiding hand of God?

1 Corinthians 13:1-13 speaks to the man who considers himself pretty successful. However, this passage tells us that speaking under the anointing of the Spirit, prophesying, or even having great faith doesn't make us an excellent person. We can do all those things and do them well, but there's a core element we must have if we want to be the "better" person. It's love, the gracious willingness to help others and put them first, that epitomizes the very nature of Jesus.

Without that level of love, no matter how well we sing in the Sunday choir, no matter how many people listen to our prophesies, and no matter who calls us great, we're still on the wrong side of our problems, and Jesus doesn't yet hold us firmly in his hand.

Let's ignore all the English teachers and better ourselves. Let's get on the good side of our problems. Let's let the love of Jesus carry his message of salvation unto the entire world.

Jesus is our number one authority, and the only thing he tells us to do is love one another.

Light Bulb Moment

When we walk in the power of Jesus, the world around us will be recharged with the power of his name.

High-Voltage Christianity

POWER LINES are amazing. They run overhead, perfectly safe, carrying massive amounts of electricity from the power plant to our houses. We can even touch the power poles holding them in the air, and we can walk away uninjured.

However, the voltages carried in those wires are so deadly they cannot be run directly to our homes. The voltages must be stepped down at a substation before we dare attach anything to the lines.

Yet, used correctly, high-voltage power lines provide air conditioning, refrigeration, and battery-charging capabilities to millions of people.

God wants us to be high-voltage Christians for him. Read of his plan in 2 Corinthians 5:20:

"Therefore, we are ambassadors for Christ, God making his appeal through us. We implore you on behalf of Christ, be reconciled to God."

God is the high voltage running through us, the same power that in the distant past formed the earth and the moon with the breath of his mouth. He melted the rocks and reformed them into what he wished them to become. He waved his hand, and the waters in the sea pressed the land aside. He touched the soil of the earth, and Man walked among God's creation.

He wants to flow through us to the world. He wants us to be his high-voltage transmission lines, walking through life buzzing with the intensity of God's awesome majesty. He wants us so charged up that he has to step down the power so we don't burn the souls of the sinners who need God in their lives.

God wants us to live a life of high-voltage Christianity, one that provides healing, comfort, and renewal to the millions of people who don't yet know him. How can we know if we're walking in the true power of God? His Word gives us the answer in 1 Corinthians 13:1-13:

"If I speak in the tongues of men and of angels, but have not love, I am a noisy gong or a clanging cymbal. And if I have prophetic powers, and understand all mysteries and all knowledge, and if I have all faith, so as to remove mountains, but have not love, I am nothing. If I give away all I have, and if I deliver up my body to be burned, but have not love, I gain nothing. Love is patient and kind; love does not envy or boast; it is not arrogant or rude. It does not insist on its own way; it is not irritable or resentful . . ."

Let's spread the power all across this world! The power is called love.

When we walk in the power of Jesus, the world around us will be recharged with the power of his name.

Light Bulb Moment

When God confirms our identity, we become someone of incalculable worth.

Identity Confirmed

A SPY'S true strength is in his anonymity. He must be able to step into any situation, complete his assignment, and step out again, never recognized for exactly who he is.

He must be able to disappear into the woodwork, to be swallowed into the crowd, to become invisible against a sea of faces.

Yet, when he contacts his superiors, he must be clearly identifiable, leaving no doubt that he is who he says he is. The spy must be able to prove he is who he claims to be.

Paul was a man of many faces. Oh, we do not see him that way now, for we have had two thousand years to define just who this man was. However, in A.D. 64, he was still living out the life of the person we now know as one of the greatest Apostles of all time.

Paul's contemporaries did not have the advantage of two millennia to give them the perspective we have today. Paul was under pressure to make his identity clear each and every time he communicated with his fellow believers. In Colossians 1:1, Paul begins his epistle by laying out his credentials in three clear proofs.

Identity Proof #1: Paul, an Apostle of Jesus Christ . . .

> To us, with millennia of hindsight at our disposal, this statement is obvious. However, in the Early Church, this was not accepted by everyone. Paul had to make his position clear. The church is led by the Holy Spirit. Paul had received the revelation of grace through the Spirit, and it was through this authority that he could lead the church.

Identity Proof #2: Through the Will of God . . .

> The early Christians were often generous in supporting the burgeoning church. A wandering "prophet" could make good money pretending to share the Word of God.

> However, only God could place a person into the office of prophet or apostle. Man did not have

the authority to do so.

Paul wanted the proof of his authority to be God.

Identity Proof #3: And Timothy our Brother . . .

Timothy was a much younger companion to Paul, one who had been very beneficial in Paul's ministry. To associate himself with Timothy was to gain approval from those who knew and appreciated Timothy's ministry.

Paul didn't stop there. As a spy must identify himself to his superiors, so must the spy confirm the identity of those to whom he reports. Hence, Colossians 1:2, in which Paul also lays out the identity of those to whom he writes in three clear confirmations.

Identity Confirmation #1: To the Saints . . .

This phrase is a clear indication of one thing. Paul had no doubt of the heart of the Colossian brethren. Paul recognized in his words that the moment a person accepts Christ, he becomes a saint. There is no delay, no proving of "miracles," no wait time after the person dies. The acceptance of Jesus makes one a saint.

Identity Confirmation #2: And Faithful Brethren in Christ . . .

> Paul was not blind. Not all those in the body at Colosse were as invested in their Christian walk as others. Paul was writing to the faithful among the church.

Identify Confirmation #3: Which are at Colosse . . .

> This epistle was written for one body, and one only. The needs of the believers were (and are) very specific, and Paul was attuned to the individual. He knew that the message of Christ was not one-fits-all. What the Colossian body needed to hear was vastly different than what the Corinthians needed. Paul introduced his letter as such, letting the people know just whom he was writing to.

Finally, Paul could greet his audience. They knew exactly where he stood, and he had called them out for exactly who they were. The business side of his introductions was cleared out of the way, and the real message could start.

> "Grace be unto you, and peace, from God our Father and the Lord Jesus Christ."

Paul knew where his strength lay. It flowed from

the Name of the Father, the Son, and the Spirit. Without them, he had no identity at all, and his life was worthless.

When God confirms our identity, we become someone of incalculable worth.

W hen we make a difference today, the effects will ripple down through the ages.

I Know Your Works

OLD CEMETERIES give the lie to our deepest desires. The names become worn, and when enough generations have come and gone, the story behind the monuments is forgotten, never to be brought to mind again.

We don't want to be forgotten. It's why we build homes, corporations, and far-reaching empires. It's why the pharaohs of old constructed the pyramids. It's why we see monuments standing in the central squares of cities across the world. If no one remembers us, then what was the point in our lives?

Yet, we can find comfort when we consider the end we must face. All that we have done is never forgotten. The Lord knows our works, and his memory is eternal. If we do our best for him, it will be remembered always, written on the walls of time itself.

Let's give our attention to Luke 14:28:

> "For which of you, desiring to build a tower, does not first sit down and count the cost, whether he has enough to complete it?"

> God wants us to "chill" a bit. We need to remember what's important. It's not being remembered in a hundred years. It's making the world around us better that counts in his eyes.

We can look to Jeremiah 29:11 for confirmation of God's good will for our lives:

> "For I know the plans I have for you, declares the Lord, plans for welfare and not for evil, to give you a future and a hope."

> The future will be what it will be. It's the present that should concern us. If we disregard today and only look to tomorrow, we have missed out on what is important in our daily walk with God. People live in the now, and only by focusing on the now can we find fulfillment in all that we do.

Job 42:10 shows the importance of looking out for our fellow man:

> "And the Lord restored the fortunes of Job, when he had prayed for his friends. And the Lord

gave Job twice as much as he had before."

The story of Job, with everything he lost, and all that was restored to him, resonates with mankind to this day. This verse tells us Job's turning point, for when he focused his prayers on his fellow man, that's when God chose to bless Job once again.

A hundred years after we are gone from this earthly life, God may be the only one who still knows the important things we did, and that's okay. He writes our deeds on the scroll of eternity, and we are never forgotten there.

When we make a difference today, the effects will ripple down through the ages.

Light Bulb Moment

Love is what allows us to repair the damage when life batters our relationships.

Linked by Love

A TRUCK and a trailer are two completely different things. Obviously. Yet, we mate them together to create something better than we had before. Here are some examples:

- ➢ We create a tractor-trailer rig, and we can ship goods across the country.
- ➢ We purchase an RV, and we can tow our home with us.
- ➢ We attach a toy hauler to our off-road vehicle, and we have our sports gear at hand.
- ➢ We hook up a new bass boat, and we can leave the land behind and head out across open water.

All of these are possible because of what we mate to our truck. Without our trailer, we couldn't do any of these things.

And if we should lose our trailer while on the road?

It's unthinkable. What's the point in our travels, if our hitch comes undone and we are forced to leave our trailer behind? The solution is linking our truck and trailer with a safety chain.

A safety chain is an extra measure of security that keeps us firmly hitched together. If something happens to break the connection holding our tow vehicle to the trailer, the safety chain keeps the link in place long enough for us to reseat the connection and get back on the road again.

In life, we are that truck and trailer. A man is very different from a woman, and yet the two are perfectly suited for each other. In a marriage, two people open up a wide world of possibilities that would be unavailable otherwise. They are linked together, and their safety chain is love.

Hebrews 13:4 gives us our marriage safety chain:

> "Let marriage be held in honor among all, and let the marriage bed be undefiled, for God will judge the sexually immoral and adulterous."

We will hit bumps, and our connection with our spouse will be tested. We can count on it. No one gets the perfect road. There will be potholes of temptation, tall mountains of adversity, and blind corners we won't see coming. When the strain on our relationship breaks us apart, it's the love that's our safety chain, giving us time to reconnect the hitch and get back on the road.

Love is what allows us to repair the damage when life batters our relationships.

Light Bulb Moment

What we respect is clear to the world. If we respect the Word of God, the world will know.

Living Bald-Headed for God

HOW DO we respect something that is lost? Do we wear white, as we might see in India, or as the daughters of Queen Juliana of the Netherlands did in 2004? Or do we don our black robes, as does much of the world to show our loss to others?

It's accepted that we grieve for all sorts of things: jobs; homes; position; people. The grieving process is designed to give us time to transition through our loss, as well as to let others know we are in pain. It's a way of respecting that which is taken from us.

Even if we choose to wear no special colors at all, those around us can tell. It's impossible hide our deepest emotion from those who know us well.

What does the Bible say about our display of respect? How can we reflect a sense of connection for that which carries importance to us?

Micah 1:16 tells us:

> "Make yourselves bald and cut off your hair, for the children of your delight; make yourselves as bald as the eagle, for they shall go from you into exile."

> If we hide our distress, how will the world know we care? Our bald head will not bring our lost loved ones back, but others will see our love for them is undiminished.

Acts 18:18 tells us:

> "After this, Paul stayed many days longer and then took leave of the brothers and set sail for Syria, and with him Priscilla and Aquila. At Cenchreae he had cut his hair, for he was under a vow."

> We aren't told Paul's vow, but it's certain he only cut his hair once he completed the vow. The people around him would then know Paul took his vows seriously. His baldness made it real to the rest of the world.

Isaiah 22:12 tells us:

> "In that day the Lord God of hosts called for weeping and mourning, for baldness and wear-

ing sackcloth."

Judah had made herself strong but without considering God's place in her fortifications. Her baldness was to be an outward sign of her coming repentance.

What does our bald head show to the world? What do we grieve for? Is it our children, carried off by the wiles of the world? Or is there a promise we have made to God? Or maybe, just maybe, our bald head is a sign of our grief for sin and our repentance before God.

We don't have to be bald headed for the world to see where we stand. It's plain in how we live, the places we visit, and the television shows we watch in our living rooms. We may think we are fooling everyone, but our bald heads are out there for everyone to see.

What we respect is clear to the world. If we respect the Word of God, the world will know.

Light Bulb Moment

Jesus loves us, this we know. Now to others, we must let it show.

Lost in Translation

HOW MANY times have we cried out in pain and anger, "I don't want anything to do with them," and all because of some wrongdoing someone has done to us?

We might later say we're sorry, but all the while, the black shadow of our hurt clouds our words. What we say isn't what we mean. It's like a foreign language, one with sounds that are familiar, but our words' intent burns the soul.

Let's picture Christ in our situation. Let's take off our shoes, hand them to him, and see what steps he would take down our angry road.

The answer might surprise us, or maybe we know already, and we just don't want to let the storm clouds dissipate.

Christ loved us enough that he gave his life for our

forgiveness. And, to think we feel that we can't forgive someone here on earth.

Colossians 1:14 is the lynchpin we need to base our attitude toward others on. In this verse, we can see the truth found in God's Word, a truth Christ shared with us on the cross, and one we are commanded to share with our fellow man:

> "In Whom we have redemption through His blood, the forgiveness of our sins."

Read that again, and then read it one more time. Then, for good measure, say it out loud while looking in the mirror.

We are to forgive!

We must ask God to forgive us for our wrongdoings, and then we must also forgive others for what they've done to us. When we truly forgive, the hurt, frustration, anger, and sadness will be gone when we remember what they've done.

Not only do we need to forgive others, we also need to forgive ourselves. That can be even more difficult to do.

Not forgiving others as well as ourselves brings on stress, sickness, pain, heartache, and loss of friendship and family.

If we feel someone owes us an apology, talk to them (and listen to what they're saying); it may be just a misunderstanding.

If we have trouble coming up with a prayer of forgiveness, Matthew 6:9-13 gives us an example we can follow:

> "Our Father Who art in heaven, hallowed be thy name.
>
> "Thy kingdom come, thy will be done on earth as it is in heaven.
>
> "Give us this day our daily bread.
>
> "And forgive us our debts, as we forgive our debtors.
>
> "And lead us not into temptation, but deliver us from the evil one.
>
> "For thine is the kingdom and the power and the glory forever.
>
> "Amen."

This is a passage we've heard and quoted many times over. If we just mouth the words as quickly as we can, the meaning will be lost in translation. We need to say it like we mean it and take the message to heart.

Jesus loves us, this we know. Now to others, we must let it show.

Light Bulb Moment

In the arms of Jesus, we can stand tall before the world.

One for Jesus; Jesus for All

THERE'S A phrase we've heard and probably said: United we stand; divided we fall. We often mean this to say if we work together, we'll get the job completed. If a few slough off, then the final result will be less than satisfactory.

This applies to family unity, too. We might fight within our family, but heaven help anyone who steps into the fray. We pull a wall around our siblings that others aren't allowed to cross.

We've heard of the military closing its ranks. If an outside attack comes against one of their own, they protect him or her at any cost. Police forces do the same. Teachers, doctors . . . we want to protect those who are bonded with us.

Colossians 3:11 says there is no Greek or Jew, no circumcised or uncircumcised, barbarian, Scythian, slave, or free. It's all Christ.

Jesus is our wall. He's the one that forms the boundary that none can be allowed to trespass. We may not agree with other Christians over doctrinal differences, but our Christ is the same. We must close ranks and protect our own.

Galatians 3:28 goes even further, for this verse tells us there is no male or female, for we are all one in Christ.

Christ sees us as sons and daughters in the same way a parent would see us as sons and daughters. Equal but different. Different but equal. In Christ we are not unisex, but equally of value in God's eyes. When he hands out the responsibilities, he does it equally. When the rewards come out, everyone gets their share.

Ephesians 6:9 tells us we each have a master, no matter what our position is in this life. Our heavenly master sees us equally, never putting one above the other.

When we see others in the faith doing mighty things for God, remember what's really important to us. It's not the big house or the jet-set lifestyle that fulfills us. It's someone holding the door, the roses when it's our birthday, and the understanding we receive when we aren't the person Christ wishes us to be. God may use the evangelist to win her thousands, but he wants to use us to win our neighbors. We are all in this for Jesus, and when we work together, Jesus is in it for us.

That familiar phrase carries a great deal of truth: United we really do stand; and if we become divided, we will come crashing to the ground.

In the arms of Jesus, we can stand tall before the world.

Light Bulb Moment

Christianity is not Winner Takes All. We find our success as a team.

Punching Up the Package

OUR CHRISTIANITY is a package deal. We can't pick financial blessings and ignore the mistreatment of our fellow man. We can't claim heaven as our home and forget that there are people still going to hell.

Yet the religious world thinks nothing of arguing church dogma and religious precepts that differ only slightly from denomination to denomination.

Even Catholic to Protestant . . . we all believe in the same Christ.

We need to punch up the package. That means we need to tout the triumph of the entire deal. We need to raise Jesus high and let the arguments slip away unnoticed.

How important does God consider this? Let's look at ten examples from his Word:

Example #1:

2 Timothy 2:14 tells us: "Remind them of these things, and charge them before God not to quarrel about words, which does no good, but only ruins the hearers."

Winning the argument is for our edification only. God's kingdom receives no satisfaction at all from our victory.

Example #2:

2 Timothy 2:16 cautions us: "But avoid irreverent babble, for it will lead people into more and more ungodliness."

The current soap opera drama or neighborhood gossip is not good subject matter, not if we want to remain close to God.

Example #3:

2 Timothy 2:23-25 says: "Have nothing to do with foolish, ignorant controversies; you know that they breed quarrels. And the Lord's servant must not be quarrelsome but kind to everyone, able to teach, patiently enduring evil, correcting his opponents with gentleness. God may perhaps grant them repentance leading to a

knowledge of the truth."

Quarreling brings no one to Jesus. Rather, it drives them away.

Example #4:

James 4:1-3 questions: "What causes quarrels and what causes fights among you? Is it not this, that your passions are at war within you? You desire and do not have, so you murder. You covet and cannot obtain, so you fight and quarrel. You do not have, because you do not ask. You ask and do not receive, because you ask wrongly, to spend it on your passions."

Rather than argue with each other, we should turn to God with our words, for he has all the final answers.

Example #5:

2 Corinthians 10:5 gives us focus: "We destroy arguments and every lofty opinion raised against the knowledge of God, and take every thought captive to obey Christ."

When we compare the arguments of this world against the Bible, all dissention will fade away. Only the Word carries the ultimate truth.

Example #6:

Proverbs 21:9 offers us a humorous comparison: "It is better to live in a corner of the housetop than in a house shared with a quarrelsome wife."

The lesson we can learn from this? If we persist in arguing, we will drive people from the church and from Jesus.

Example #7:

Proverbs 15:1 is our solution: "A soft answer turns away wrath, but a harsh word stirs up anger."

We can't afford to cave in to wrong thinking just for the sake of peace. Neither can we confront misconceptions with a strong hand. Rather, we must gently present the truth.

Example #8:

1 Timothy 6:4 describes the argumentative man: "He is puffed up with conceit and understands nothing. He has an unhealthy craving for controversy and for quarrels about words, which produce envy, dissension, slander, evil suspicions."

This is a mirror we can hold up to ourselves. How do we compare?

Example #9:

James 1:19 speaks to those on both sides of the argument: "Know this, my beloved brothers: let every person be quick to hear, slow to speak, slow to anger."

It takes two to argue. It also takes two to slow down and discuss a subject peacefully.

Example #10:

Matthew 7:3 shows just how ludicrous arguing really is: "Why do you see the speck that is in your brother's eye, but do not notice the log that is in your own eye?"

No one is perfect. We just tend to overlook our own imperfections and yet hold others to impossible standards.

Not only is Christianity a package deal, so are the people who walk the straight and narrow way at our side. When we punch up the package, we become a support network for one another. We encourage stragglers in times of difficulty, correct misunderstandings with gentle words, and always,

always stand by those who endeavor to do right in the sight of the Lord.

Christianity is not Winner Takes All. We find our success as a team.

Light Bulb Moment

Jesus is our purple and fine linen. Any other source of pride brings us to a bad ending.

Purple and Fine Linen

TYRIAN PURPLE is the color of kings.

There was a time that wearing purple was forbidden by law, unless you were royalty. It was as much a symbol of elevated status as a crown on the head of a prince.

It cost about as much, too. Why? We have to look to why it's called Tyrian purple to learn that.

In Lebanon, near the city of Tyre, marine mollusks were harvested by vast quantities to extract the gland that becomes the royal purple color. It was time intensive, painfully hard, and vastly expensive to produce the dye that saturated the fabrics that graced the limbs of Roman emperors and European kings.

It was a symbol that the wearer was better than the average Joe, and that others had better step aside.

Today we don't cotton to that attitude, and for good reason. We understand color is not an indication of status. Rather, it is an indicator of taste and preference.

Luke 16:19-31 tells the story of the rich man and Lazarus, a poor beggar. Lazarus was covered with sores, while the rich man dressed in purple and fine linen.

The rich man thought his purple and fine linen made him better than the beggar just outside his door that ate from his scraps.

What does the Word tell us?

Matthew 25:41 tells us God will divide the left from the right:

> "Then he will say to those on his left, 'Depart from me, you cursed, into the eternal fire prepared for the devil and his angels.' "

Matthew 25:46 names our punishment or reward:

> "And these will go away into eternal punishment, but the righteous into eternal life."

Revelation 20:10 warns us we are responsible for our fellow traveler:

"And the devil who had deceived them was thrown into the lake of fire and sulfur where the beast and the false prophet were, and they will be tormented day and night forever and ever."

Jude 1:6 says no one is exempt from the hand of God:

"And the angels who did not stay within their own position of authority, but left their proper dwelling, he has kept in eternal chains under gloomy darkness until the judgment of the great day—"

1 John 5:17 makes it clear we can choose a better way:

"All wrongdoing is sin, but there is sin that does not lead to death."

The question we have to face is one men have faced for countless generations. Do we choose purple and fine linen, or do we choose the Lord? That question has nothing to do with the clothes we wear, but rather with how we view ourselves in our walk through this life. Do we consider ourselves above God's laws? Do we look down our noses at those around us who struggle to do right? Or do we find our righteousness in the Lord?

The end of the passage in Luke 16:19-31 tells of the rich man in torment, and the beggar in Abraham's arms. Which man got what he deserved?

Will we get what we deserve? Let's draw close to God, and trust him to one day ferry us home to be with our Lord for all time.

Jesus is our purple and fine linen. Any other source of pride brings us to a bad ending.

Light Bulb Moment

When God knows he can trust us, he will recommend us to the people of the world.

Refer-a-Friend

WIN A $10 gift card! All we have to do is refer a friend to the latest sales program. Netflix will give us a month free for every friend we refer. Dropbox? Extra cloud storage space. Scottrade? Free online stock market trades. Online gaming? Points, bonus levels, and extra lives.

Friend referrals are one of the most beneficial ways of advertising that any company can use. It's free, it's sincere, and most of all, there is an emotional link between the friend and the product. The interest in the product comes from the connection with the friend, and because of that, it is stronger, even before product has actually changed hands.

In a job interview, we call this a letter of recommendation. Without one, that job offer may evaporate with our first interview question. With one, we are a shoo-in for the job.

Paul understood this implicitly. He knew that tapping his network of friendships and associations would spread the gospel faster and farther than if unknown people carried the story of Christ, no matter how good their message.

In the book of Colossians, Paul writes to a church he has never visited. They are being led astray by false teachings. He knows people who can steer them the right direction, so he refers those friends to the church at Colosse.

We can read his recommendations in Colossians 4:7-14.

Let's look at the people in Paul's Refer-a-Friend program:

Tychicus.

> Paul uses two words to describe Tychicus: beloved and faithful.
>
> Tychicus was particularly valued by Paul. He served as Paul's courier, hand-delivering letters and messages, and fielding questions about Paul's imprisonment.

Onesimus.

Paul uses the same two words to describe Onesimus: beloved and faithful.

However, Onesimus carries a special recommendation. Onesimus is a runaway slave who has come to know Christ as his savior. Paul especially treasured Onesimus, and he desired Onesimus' brotherhood in Christ to supersede his position as a runaway slave.

Aristarchus.

Paul describes Aristarchus as his fellow prisoner.

Aristarchus, a Greek from Thessalonica, is also mentioned in various verses in Acts and in the book of Philemon. After a rough time at Ephesus, Aristarchus accompanied Paul in his travels to Macedonia and Palestine, and later to Rome. Aristarchus was Paul's right arm.

Marcus.

Paul gives Marcus his highest praise.

Marcus, or John Mark, had once been at odds with Paul, causing a rift between Paul and his companion Barnabas so great that the men never ministered together again. However, Marcus soon rose to meet Paul's expectations, eventually penning the Gospel of Mark in the New Testament.

Jesus, called Justus.

Paul includes Jesus, called Justus, in his most select circle of friends.

Paul names Jesus Justus as a fellow Jew, one of three, including Aristarchus and Mark, who had been a comfort to him. Jesus, also called the Christ, came first to the Jews. Those of the Jewish faith who found their hope in Jesus Christ were especially treasured by Paul.

Epaphras.

Paul calls Epaphras a servant of Christ.

In Paul's eyes, there was no greater honor to bestow on a fellow believer. Epaphras was a mighty prayer warrior, conspicuous in his perseverance for Christ. Epaphras carried a zeal for the spiritual welfare of others.

Luke.

Luke, a great friend of Paul, the writer of the third canonical gospel, needs no introduction to the modern church.

In the same vein, Paul's referral gives little information about his friend, other than to describe him as a beloved physician. The bond between the two men was evidently well-known. This is the same Luke who was with Paul during his last days at Mamertine prison in Rome, where Paul wrote his second and final missive to Timothy.

Demas.

Demas faithfully served alongside Paul in Rome, and Paul recommends him to the body at Colosse.

However, later, in 2 Timothy, Paul would reveal Demas' desertion when he abandoned Paul's ministry, making it clear that following Christ is a choice. Comfort and wealth meant more to Demas than the advancement of the gospel of Christ. Demas becomes Paul's greatest disappointment and most heartfelt failure.

Paul opened the doors of Colosse to these men. His letter of recommendation put them in the enviable position of not having to prove themselves to the believers there.

These were men who had already proved themselves to the Lord.

When God knows he can trust us, he will recommend us to the people of the world.

Light Bulb Moment

When we run with Jesus, it's springtime all the time. He is the sunshine that gives us life, filling us with the warmth of his love.

Running With Jesus

WE LOOK forward to spring.

It's a time of sunshine, warmth, renewed life, and brighter tomorrows.

Part of it is simply getting outdoors. We visit the park, the grass is freshly green, and we can run with abandon, soaking it all in. Children chase each other, we toss balls to our dogs, and birds chatter cheerfully in the trees.

Who wouldn't want to run in the park on a bright spring day? It's a renewal of self, of life, of all the things we need to make us happy. It's a way of recharging after a winter of being indoors.

Drawing close to God is like finding ourselves in the park on a beautiful afternoon. We want to throw our arms in the air and run with abandon toward him.

John 4:24 says:

> "God is spirit, and those who worship him must worship in spirit and truth."

> Whoo-whoo! Let's lift our arms toward the sunshine!

Romans 3:23 tells us:

> "For all have sinned and fall short of the glory of God."

> Wahoo! That was then, but it's us no longer!

John 3:16 shows us the sunshine of his love:

> "For God so loved the world, that he gave his only Son, that whoever believes in him should not perish but have eternal life."

> Glory! Spring has arrived, and we can soak up his warmth!

John 1:1 warms our faces:

> "In the beginning was the Word, and the Word was with God, and the Word was God."

> Whoop! Whoop! God's been there all along!

Revelation 1:17-18 says our spring day in the park shall never end:

> "Fear not, I am the first and the last, and the living one. I died, and behold I am alive forevermore, and I have the keys of Death and Hades."

> Frisbee time! Jesus is in total control!

Titus 2:13 assures us our Lord will join us:

> "[We are] waiting for our blessed hope, the appearing of the glory of our great God and Savior Jesus Christ."

> Break out the fried chicken! We're about to feast!

John 14:6 is our park day agenda:

> "Jesus said to him, 'I am the way, and the truth, and the life. No one comes to the Father except through me.'"

> All right! Let's get with the program!

John 1:3 says the entire park is the domain of Christ:

> "All things were made through him, and without him was not any thing made that was made."

Hot dog! All of creation is ours to play in all day long!

When we run with Jesus, it's springtime all the time. He is the sunshine that gives us life, filling us with the warmth of his love.

Light Bulb Moment

Taking time to keep ourselves strong in God is worth a little of our effort. Our families will be better for it.

Setting Up Our Wall

BUNKER MENTALITY is sometimes all we have left. We must put up a wall for protection from the wiles of the evil one.

In its simplest form, we turn off the phone to keep telemarketers from bothering us at dinner. Our vacations are often a way of running away from the pressures of the world even if it's only for a week.

Sometimes it's as easy as a walk to cool down after emotional fisticuffs with our spouse. We need a wall to allow us a time of separation before reengaging with the world.

Nehemiah was generous with the Jews. He rebuilt the walls of Jerusalem. He did it at his own expense. Others tried to destroy him for his good deeds, and God took exception, keeping his hand on Nehemiah.

We need to follow Nehemiah's example. When we find a breach in that which protects us, it's up to us to break out the building tools and repair our walls. Our marriages, our families, they are our responsibility. It's not up to the minster, the marriage counselor, or the social worker to fix what's wrong with our lives. We need to raise our wall, protect what God has given us, and work to make right that which we are blessed with.

No one gets that vacation without booking the trip and paying the bill.

Nehemiah 6:15-16 tells us:

> "So the wall was finished on the twenty-fifth day of the month Elul, in fifty-two days. And when all our enemies heard of it, all the nations around us were afraid and fell greatly in their own esteem, for they perceived that this work had been accomplished with the help of our God."

Our walls of protection will bring about the same result for us. When we set up our wall around that which is important to us, we will grow stronger, and the evil one will be afraid of what God had brought forth in us.

Taking time to keep ourselves strong in God is

worth a little of our effort. Our families will be better for it.

Finding beauty in God makes the world's beauty pale in comparison.

The Beautiful Sin

WORLD TRAVELERS are a unique breed, a people who reach out to grasp the beauty that our world offers. From the sweeping mountain vistas of Bavaria to sun-drenched Mexico, who would not travel the world if money were no object?

How can we see such beauty and not want to take it all in?

2 Samuel 11:2 tells of a king who did just that. He looked out upon a sweeping landscape, and beauty filled his vision. He discovered he wanted to reach out for it no matter what it cost.

> "It happened, late one afternoon, when David arose from his couch and was walking on the roof of the king's house, that he saw from the roof a woman bathing; and the woman was very beautiful."

We know the story of David and Bath-sheba, a

woman of great beauty who was already married to another man. David was drawn to her beauty, and he committed a sin against God and Bath-sheba.

It was a sin of great beauty, and in its moment of consummation, David probably enjoyed it very much. However, the results were a good man David brought to his death, manipulating Bath-sheba's husband Uriah on the battlefield so that he was killed. Then the child born of David's sin sickened and died.

David was that world traveler who had the means to reach out and possess all the beauty the world had to offer. Uriah had claimed one small part of the beauty for his own, and David took it. The beauty he beheld with his eyes became a sin unto him, and it was beautiful no more.

Matthew 5:28 tells us:

> "But I say to you that everyone who looks at a woman with lustful intent has already committed adultery with her in his heart."

2 Timothy 2:22 encourages us:

> "So flee youthful passions and pursue righteousness, faith, love, and peace, along with those who call on the Lord from a pure heart."

Galatians 5:24 gives us our goal:

> "And those who belong to Christ Jesus have crucified the flesh with its passions and desires."

David was consumed with passion, and it twisted on him, turning his moment of satisfaction into a time of untold sorrow. 1 Corinthians 6:20 tells us we are bought with a price, and we are to glorify God in our bodies.

So, what are we to take from this? God gives us beauty in this world to provide us enjoyment. However, there are lines in the sand that speak of what's available to us and what's not. If we cross one of those lines, the backlash is greater than the beauty ever was.

Finding beauty in God makes the world's beauty pale in comparison.

Light Bulb Moment

When we carve God into our problems, even our problems will become a witness unto him.

The Hand-Carved Beam

WE KNOW that saying about lemons. When life throws them at us, don't get distressed over their sour taste. Rather, we need to slice them up, and bask in the sun with our glass of lemonade in hand.

What we're really saying is make the most of whatever situation we're in. If we can't change what's wrong with our life, then find the best way to look at it, and focus on that.

Matthew 7:1-5 speaks to this in a slightly different way. We are told not to speak in judgment about other people unless we've removed the bigger transgression from our own life.

The problem we face sometimes runs deeper. That log in our eye that prevents us from helping our brother is sometimes all we can see. How then can we help those around us who are in need?

John 7:24 tells us to "judge with right judgment." Essentially this means to look deeper than what we can see. We have to judge with the purity of Christ.

If we can't remove the log, and it's all we can see, let's make lemonade out of it. Let's carve it with the Word of God, sculpt our Christian witness into its surface, and shape it to look like Christ. Let's turn that mighty obstruction into a hand-carved beam filled with the love of God, and soon, the love of Christ will be all that we can see.

Once we've done that, others will look at us, and they won't see a great obstruction obscuring our vision. They'll see the mighty gifts of God flowing from us, and obscuring the evils of the world from our sight.

We will be the witness to the lost that Jesus wishes us to be. We will emulate our Lord, because that will be all we can see.

When we carve God into our problems, even our problems will become a witness unto him.

Light Bulb Moment

If we want to exemplify Jesus, let's think of ways to show our love to those we meet each and every day.

The Sparrow's Wingbeat

SPARROWS ARE small birds, with wingspans about the size of an opened hand, and short, stubby beaks. They are certainly the most familiar of wild birds, because they nest where humanity lives.

If we build it, they will come.

If we build what, who will come? The sparrow, of course. They tend to nest on buildings and under the eaves of houses, putting them right at our fingertips, no matter where we are. When we expand our cities, the sparrow's buildable habitat expands, also.

We live side by side with this adaptable bird. It also means we cannot get away from it. If we are there, it is at our side. It is for that reason Ecclesiastes 10:20 uses a bird to bring its warning home:

"Even in your thoughts, do not curse the king,

nor in your bedroom curse the rich, for a bird of the air will carry your voice, or some winged creature tell the matter."

Ecclesiastes is attributed to Solomon, meaning it was written some 3,000 years ago. If mankind needed to be careful then, how much more true is that now? With email records, security cameras, and personal cell phones recording everything we say and do, if we say it or even think it, it will get out. Our curses will be made known.

We should look instead to Philippians 4:8 for a better way:

> "Finally, brothers, whatever is true, whatever is honorable, whatever is just, whatever is pure, whatever is lovely, whatever is commendable, if there is any excellence, if there is anything worthy of praise, think about these things."

Even the secular world knows we become what we think. It's the reason there are so many "life coaches" who espouse positive thinking. If we think in a positive manner, we will change our outlook on life, and in the process, we will change the outcome of our day-to-day actions. We will live better.

1 Corinthians 13:13 is our power of positive think-

ing focus:

> "So now faith, hope, and love abide, these three; but the greatest of these is love."

When we think on love, the sparrow's wingbeats will carry that to every household in our neighborhood. Why? When we think on love, we will change our outlook on life, and in the process, we will change our interactions with those around us. We will live better, and our fellow man will reap the benefits of our love for him.

If we want to exemplify Jesus, let's think of ways to show our love to those we meet each and every day.

Light Bulb Moment

We are woven into a whole by the hand of Jesus. It is the resulting tapestry that is beautiful.

The Weaving Machine

FABRIC DOES NOT come from a fabric tree. A woven tapestry does not grow from a tapestry seed, blooming into a beautiful creation on our wall. The coarsest cotton cloth has to be crafted from individual threads, one piece at a time.

Centuries ago, this was done by hand, each layer woven into the whole in a tedious, finger-numbing process that often took weeks to complete. Larger works? The timeframe could run to months or even years.

Today cloth is pumped out on massive weaving machines, giant automated automatons that work tirelessly day and night to produce the intricate fabrics that surround our every waking moment. Without these weaving machines, our lives would be coarser, poorer, and much less enjoyable. Centuries ago we might have owned one set of clothes, been lucky to have a sheet for our mattress, and a towel? Good luck there. Today we have closets stuffed full of textiles that only a king could have afforded in those days.

Our Christian life is one giant tapestry. Our weaving machine is God the Father in heaven, and we are his threads. He weaves us together in an intricate fashion, choosing just which threads go where, in order to create the most beautiful image possible.

We can see God's weaving machine in action in Colossians 3:18-25. In this passage, Paul describes each thread in the tapestry and exactly where God needs it to go. If we follow God's plan, we will become beautiful in him.

The Thread of Domestic Life:

> In Paul's day and time, women working outside of the home was more unusual than not. What we term "domestic life" was very labor intensive. A woman could not set the dishwasher for midnight, throw in a load of laundry before breakfast, and turn the vacuum on to automatically sweep the floors sometime during the afternoon.
>
> Women were tied to household duties and also

to their husbands. Knowing this, Paul instructs wives to submit themselves to their husbands. However, this by no means suggests lying down and being a doormat. Paul makes this clear when he explains in no uncertain terms that his words are only for those women whose husbands function in the spirit of the Lord.

The Thread Called Husbands:

Husbands and wives were held to different standards in the first century. A man had rights and privileges that a woman did not possess. Generally, although there were differences in actual practice, if a man found anything about his wife that was unacceptable, he could divorce her, and once divorced she was branded. No one would marry her. A wife had no such recourse, except in the most heinous of situations.

Paul compared the love of a husband toward his wife with the love that we offer unto God. We may not agree with God, may even become disgruntled with God, but we do not divorce God. Men are to be the same with their wives. Husbands are not to cast their wives aside carelessly. We must be there through thick and thin, and it is our love that will smooth the rough places.

The Children Thread:

Children do not grow up with a strong sense of values as an innate and intrinsic part of their core being. Values are not instinctual. They are learned. The crux is that the values children learn in the home are the same values that transfer to their adult lives and into their relationship with God.

Paul lays out his instructions for children in much the same way as he lays out his instructions for wives. He says, obey your parents in all things. Remember, though, Paul is writing to the church at Colosse, not to a pagan tribe in Britain or North Africa. When parents function in the spirit of the Lord, they present good models for their children to emulate. It is pleasing to God when children emulate and obey their parents in all good things.

The Fathers Thread:

The men of the household had all the power. Legally, men bought and sold, could marry and divorce, and when family property changed hands? The man's fingers were all over it.

Paul does not tell fathers what to do. Culturally,

in the timeframe in which Paul wrote this letter, fathers could do almost anything they wanted. Instead, Paul goes at this from a different angle, telling fathers what not to do. When Paul tells fathers to be careful and not provoke their children to anger, what he is really saying is that we must build our children's respect with love and praise. If they only fear us, that will transfer into their adult lives, and we will paralyze their effectiveness to the Lord.

The Thread of Servants Everywhere:

Slavery was a reality in the first century, and a portion of those in the Early Church were in legal bondage to other men. Paul did not dispute the realities of his day. Rather, he advised that even slaves had a duty before the Lord, to present themselves in the light of the teachings of Christ.

In the modern world, we may not be legal slaves, but we find ourselves faced with many of the same situations Paul pointed out in this passage. We are not to do our jobs when the boss is watching, but play on our computers when he is away. If we do wrong against our employers, it will come back on us. We represent Christ, not only in our homes, but in our places of employment, too.

Paul winds up this passage telling us that even while God understands that we all have different roles in life, he does not hold one position up as more important than another. God does not play favorites, just because one is a wife, a husband, a child, a father, or a slave. We are all threads in his tapestry.

While we are all made from different threads, God uses each of us to weave this tapestry of life. If we play our parts carefully and faithfully, it will be beautiful.

We are woven into a whole by the hand of Jesus. It is the resulting tapestry that is beautiful.

Light Bulb Moment

If the only rule we live by is the Golden Rule, then we will live well.

Tit for Tat

WHAT GOES around comes around; live and let live; do unto others what you would have them do unto you.

These are all phrases for equality; for fair treatment of our fellow man; for living well, yet not living well at another's expense.

Tit for tat. I'll give unto you what you gave unto me.

Normally used in a vindictive mien, this three word phrase's connotation is that of equivalent retaliation. Often used in game strategy, it simply means to respond in kind.

We see this in business with the handshake given in greeting. I reach out—tit—and you reach back—tat—in a warm and congenial manner.

However, if the meeting does not go well, and I treat you unfairly, you are justified in also treating me unfairly. For example, I strike a fair deal with you, yet months later, I undercut your pricing structure. In tit for tat, you are free to then undercut my pricing structure, and so on.

In true tit-for-tat fashion, I even expect you to do so.

Gas stations do this all the time, one lowering prices, knowing the station on the opposite corner will soon follow suit. And airlines. Anyone who flies frequently is aware of the power of the major players, from baggage fees to food service. Even daily fares for every airline can drop radically if only one offers severe discounts.

Tit for tat is biblical, and directly from the mouth of Jesus. We can find his words in Matthew 7:12, Mark 12:31, and Luke 6:31, all telling us to play fairly.

Tit for tat.

Even under the rigid constraints of the Old Covenant, Leviticus 19:18 says not to bear a grudge or take your vengeance on another, but to love that person as you do the one who looks back at you out of the mirror.

Paul addresses this issue very specifically in Colossians 4:1. He is speaking to slave owners, but his words are to us.

The masters of slaves in Paul's day owned them hoof and hind; there were few laws restricting how they were to be treated. Only the most heinous and brutal treatment was condemned.

A Roman slave could not even speak up for himself in a court of law.

Yet Paul encourages tit for tat. Do unto others what you would have them do unto you.

Paul says it this way: Masters, give unto your servants good and fair treatment . . .

Yet, those words only give us the tit. Certainly, it is right and good that the master treat his slave well, but where is the benefit for the master?

That brings us to the tat.

Paul continues: Remember, you also have a master, one who resides in heaven.

Tit for tat. What goes around comes around. Live a life well-ordered and full of mercy, and let those you interact with each day have the opportunity to live in the same manner. Treat your business partner; your neighbor; your spouse; and your children in the way that you would want to be treated.

The Word of God goes so far as to offer us some suggestions:

Tit for Tat Suggestion #1:

> Be positive. Hebrews 10:24.
>
> Tell those around us at least one good thing they've done each day. If they live far away, text it to them.

Tit for Tat Suggestion #2:

> Be patient and kind. 1 Corinthians 13:4-7.
>
> Count to three, then don't say it. Then ask if there's anything you can do to help. Then help.

Tit for Tat Suggestion #3:

> Show respect. 1 Peter 2:17.
>
> Imagine that the person next to you is your grandmother. How would you treat her?

Tit for Tat Suggestion #4:

> Be sympathetic and tenderhearted. 1 Peter 3:8.
>
> Just listen. Then don't offer advice. Listen, cry

along, and let them come back and do it again. For free.

Tit for Tat Suggestion #5:

Be merciful. Ephesians 4:32.

Put on their shoes. Have a meal with them. Get to know the person who's offended you. Then decide if you want to punish them. Finally, remember, you are wearing their shoes.

Tit for Tat Suggestion #6:

Be generous with those in need. 1 John 3:16-19.

Once a month, leave a $50 tip. In ten years, you will not remember, but that waiter always will.

Tit for Tat Suggestion #7:

Honor one another. Romans 12:10.

Cook a cake for a neighbor, simply because they live next door. Meet the postman with a water bottle. Smile, and say, this is because you are special.

If the only rule we live by is the Golden Rule, then we will live well.

Light Bulb Moment

Jesus is our leader, and he guides us to our final resting place with his heavenly words of wisdom.

Wagons Westward Ho!

AMERICAN SETTLERS in the 1800s had a lot of stuff to carry west. They had to pack enough for months on the road. Flour, sugar, dried meat, and sundry supplies weighed their wagons down. To move all that gear required massive teams of oxen yoked together.

For the oxen to pull successfully, the yoke had to be able to flex from side to side. Otherwise it would chafe the animals, and they would rebel against their drivers.

One other important thing about a successful team of oxen? They weren't driven with reins and a whip. Rather, the driver walked at their side, and the animals learned to respond to the sound of his voice. Put a strange driver in place, and the oxen no longer knew which way to go.

Five passages in Corinthians speak to the yokes we

wear as we travel through this life.

2 Corinthians 6:15 talks about the devil:

> "What accord has Christ with Belial? Or what portion does a believer share with an unbeliever?"

> Belial is literally translated as ungodliness, and is generally taken to mean the devil. If we are yoked to the devil, we'll go the wrong way every time.

2 Corinthians 6:14 refers to our attachments with our fellow man:

> "Do not be unequally yoked with unbelievers. For what partnership has righteousness with lawlessness? Or what fellowship has light with darkness?"

> If we allow those who choose wrong ways to link with us, our yoke will begin to bind, and we will rebel against God.

1 Corinthians 15:33 tells us we are more likely to be pulled away from good than towards it:

> "Do not be deceived: Bad company ruins good morals."

We can't date with disaster, hoping to pull others our way. Instead, they will lead us astray.

1 Corinthians 6:18 says temporary yokes can be deadly devices:

> "Flee from sexual immorality. Every other sin a person commits is outside the body, but the sexually immoral person sins against his own body."

Telling ourselves our indulgement is just for the moment, and that no one will know leaves the imprint of our misguided yoke on every part of our lives.

1 Corinthians 6:9 gives us our final destination if we continue to wear the yoke of sin:

> "Or do you not know that the unrighteous will not inherit the kingdom of God? Do not be deceived . . ."

We wear the yoke of Christ with an endpoint in mind. When we let the flexibility of Jesus' requirements become the liberty of wrong living, he will no longer guide us, and we will never reach our heavenly home.

Christ our Savior walks at our side, guiding us safely

toward our westward home. If we pay attention to his voice, our yoke will feel light upon our shoulders, and those at our side will lighten our burden. We will arrive as a team, achieving heaven as our destination.

Jesus is our leader, and he guides us to our final resting place with his heavenly words of wisdom.

Coming to Christ
In Three Easy Steps

If you do not know Christ as your personal savior, there is no better time than the present to turn your life over to him.

- Step 1 is to admit that you are human, God is God, and you need his grace.
- Step 2 is to place your belief in him. You must accept that he is the Son of the Eternal God, and through his death on the cross, he can give you new life.
- Step 3 is to turn from your previous ways and receive the hope of Jesus' power in you.

Fill in the following information as a testament to your decision to accept Jesus as your Savior.

I, _____, accept Jesus
       print your full name

as my personal savior on _____.
                                today's date

_____
         your signature

Look for these additional topics on the MyChurchNotes.net website:

2 Timothy
Beatitudes
Discipleship
Evangelism
Faith
Family
Healing
Hope
Kingdom of God
Money
Prayer
Relationships
Repentance
Salvation
Worship

MyChurchNotes.net is a faith-based ministry founded on a belief in the Father, the Son, and the Holy Spirit. All MyChurchNotes.net articles are based on Scripture and created especially for MyChurchNotes.net.

Our Mission Statement is to take the Word of God into all the nations, and proclaim that he is Lord!

If you enjoyed
God Renews Our Relationships with Others,
please visit us at our website:

www.MyChurchNotes.net

We look forward to hearing from you.

Website and Publication Powered by:

Bright Herd . . . for All Your Website and
Media Design Needs.
www.brightherd.com
contact@brightherd.com

www.ingramcontent.com/pod-product-compliance
Lightning Source LLC
Chambersburg PA
CBHW070639050426
42451CB00008B/226